Robots on the Move

Steve Parker

W
FRANKLIN WATTS
LONDON • SYDNEY

An Appleseed Editions book

First published in 2010 by Franklin Watts
338 Euston Road, London NW1 3BH

Franklin Watts Australia
Hachette Children's Books
Level 17/207 Kent St, Sydney, NSW 2000

© 2010 Appleseed Editions

Created by Appleseed Editions Ltd,
Well House, Friars Hill, Guestling,
East Sussex TN35 4ET

Designed by Guy Callaby
Edited by Mary-Jane Wilkins
Picture research by Su Alexander

ISBN 978 1 4451 0034 0

Dewey Classification 629.8'932

A CIP catalogue for this book is available from
the British Library.

Picture acknowledgements

Title page AFP/Getty Images; contents page John Hicks/Corbis;
4 Maximilian Stock Ltd/Science Photo Library; 5 Mode Images
Ltd/Alamy; 6 & 7 Getty Images; 8 Vaughn Youtz/Zuma/Corbis;
9t AFP/Getty Images, b Jochen Luebke/epa/Corbis;
10 Maximilian Stock Ltd/Science Photo Library; 11 Volker
Moehrke/Corbis, r Philippe Plailly/Eurelios/Science Photo
Library; 12 National Geographic/Getty Images; 13t Vaughn
Youtz/Zuma/Corbis, b Izmostock/Alamy; 14t Julian Calder/
Corbis, b Car Culture/Corbis; 15 Culture-Images GmbH/
Alamy; 16 DARPA; 17 AFP/Getty Images; 18 Getty Images;
19t Getty Images, b John Hicks/Corbis; 20 Gianni Muratore/
Alamy; 21t David Hodges/Alamy, b Photos 12/Alamy;
22 © Colin Sauze 2007; 23 Karen Kasmauski/Corbis;
24 Louie Psihoyos/Corbis; 25 Peter Ginter/Science Faction/
Corbis; 26 Chris Carroll/Corbis; 27t Jerry Lampen/Reuters/
Corbis, b Peter Ginter/Science Faction/Corbis; 28 GSFC/
NASA; 29t GSFC/NASA, b ESA-J Huart
Front cover Peter Menzel/Science Photo Library

Printed in China

Franklin Watts is a division of Hachette
Children's Books,
an Hachette UK company.
www.hachette.co.uk

Contents

Robots go!

Some robots stay in one place and can't move about. But others are rarely still. These robots go places and do things, often by themselves, without needing our help. That's partly what makes them robots.

Why travel?

Most robots have gears, motors, levers and similar moving parts inside. These whirr and spin and **pivot**. But not all robots can move themselves from place to place on wheels or legs. Robots which travel are called mobile, roving, active or **locomotory robots**.

Mobile robots move around for a reason. Designers and engineers build them to carry out particular jobs or tasks, which need them to go from one place to another. Giving a robot wheels or legs when it does not really need them would be a waste of effort, time, energy and money.

▼ Robot trucks and carriers called automated guided vehicles (AGVs) carry items around factories, stores and warehouses. They follow guide wires buried under the floor.

Energy needs

A roving robot is much more complicated than one which is stationary or fixed in one place. Not only does a mobile robot need wheels, legs or other mechanical parts to move around – it also needs the energy to move. This may come from an onboard energy source, such as a battery. The robot also needs to be able to find its way, or navigate, and to avoid bumps and crashes that might damage it or objects around it – including people. Safety is important when robots travel around.

Robot helpers

Some robots travel long distances but don't have wheels, legs or similar parts. These are onboard robots for ships, trains, planes, trucks, wagons and other vehicles. Sometimes they operate alone and are in command, with no people. In other cases the robots are partly automatic, and act as helpers for human pilots, drivers and riders.

▼ *If the human pilot switched off the radio controller, this model plane would soon crash. It cannot fly safely on its own, unlike a true robot aircraft.*

ROBOT OR NOT?
○○○

Total control

Many people play with radio-controlled (RC) model cars, trucks, planes and ships. Are these true robots? Not usually. Most move about according to the instructions of the operator, who controls their speed and direction, second by second. Real robots control themselves and work automatically to some extent.

How robots move

Humans can walk, jump, hop and run. Some robots can walk, and a very few can even run. But most robots move around in other ways. Many roll along on wheels. There are robots that trundle on rollers and rumble on crawler tracks. And there are robots with propellers that fly through the sky, swish across water or even float on air like a hovercraft.

Soryu the snake is a rescue robot with sets of crawler tracks which allow it to travel in awkward places. It searches for people at disaster sites, such as in the rubble of a collapsed building, using its video camera eye.

Wheeling along

One of the best ways for robots to move around is to roll on wheels. But wheels work best on smooth surfaces such as floors, paths and roads. They have trouble with lumpy, bumpy and softer surfaces, such as soil, leaves, sand and stones. Most wheeled robots can't go up or down a steep ramp or stairs. They have trouble even stepping over a kerbstone.

Moving at a crawl

Caterpillar tracks or crawler tracks can be an alternative to wheels for travelling over rough ground. But movement on these is slow and they need lots of power. So cat-track robots need huge batteries or a long wire connecting them to an electricity supply. Another option is to travel along rails, like a railway train. However, that limits where the robot can go.

Through air and water

For the robots that we send up into the sky, or over and under the sea, propellers are the best choice. On robo-planes the props are often called air screws, and for robot ships they are water screws. This is because their twisted blades pull them along through air or water with a screw-like movement.

The four-propeller AirRobot measures one metre across and finds its way using GPS satellite navigation. It can hover, take pictures with its three cameras, and send them back to base via radio signals. This makes it useful for checking accident scenes.

DO YOU KNOW?

(ROBOTS DO)

Travellers' tales

Adventurous people travel to many remote places, such as mountain peaks and deep caves. Some mobile robots go on even stranger journeys. They burrow through soil, squeeze through long narrow pipelines, and voyage through pitch black, freezing underground rivers or oceans. If only they could tell us about their adventures...

Robo-rolling

Making a mobile robot with wheels turned by an electric motor sounds simple. But there are hundreds of sizes and types of wheels. There are also many different types of tyres, as well as different electric motors, axles and bearings, gears, chains, steering methods... So it's not so simple.

Size matters

Big wheels move a robot faster than small wheels, if the wheels turn at the same speed. Large wheels are heavier and harder for the motor to spin, so the motor needs to be more powerful to give it greater turning force, called **torque**. Big wheels work best on smooth surfaces. Smaller wheels cope better with bumpy ground, but a small-wheeled robot can be so close to the ground that it gets stuck on bumps.

Outdoor robots need big tyres with deep treads to cover rough ground. This is Terramax, an entrant in the DARPA Challenge (see page 16).

Halluc II rolls along on eight steerable wheels, each with an electric motor. Alternatively, it can lock all the wheels and walk along like a spider.

Robo-blog ■

WORN OUT AND WEARY

'Today's work was really hard. My wheels are worn, my bearings are painful and my motor is stiff and clunky. I need a few squirts of runny oil and some blobs of sticky grease. That would make me loose and lubricated. But my human masters have forgotten. Tomorrow maybe I'll overheat and grind to a halt. That'll show them!' ■

Hard rims

A wheel with a hard plastic or metal edge, called the rim, is strong and long-lasting. The problem with hard edges is that they can slip and skid easily on many surfaces. They also give a hard, jolting ride, which might shake and damage the robot's delicate parts inside.

Softer edges

Rubber, soft plastic or spongy foam tyres are best for grip. Robots which work outside need tyres with a pattern of grooves called tread, like car or bicycle tyres. The tread grips damp, slippery surfaces well. The problem with softer tyres is that they wear out faster. If they are **pneumatic** (filled with air), like bicycle tyres, sharp objects might puncture them. Few robots can mend their own punctures or change their own wheels!

ROBOT SUPERSTAR

Blue Max

One of the biggest and best fun fighting robots is Blue Max. It weighs as much as two people and has a big, deep-tread tyre on each corner, for the best possible grip. Its main weapon is a sloping wedge at the front, which it pushes under rival robots to flip them over.

Motoring along

More than 99 of every 100 mobile robots are powered by electric motors. The size of the motor depends on the robot's weight and the load it might have to carry. Big heavy robots might have two motors, or even one for each wheel.

Gearing up for big loads

Motors have a part that spins called the drive shaft, which can turn around hundreds of times a second. A wheel fixed to the shaft would spin so fast that the robot would zoom out of control and crash! So every motor has sets of **gears** called **reduction gears**. A small toothed gear **cog** (gearwheel) on the motor's driveshaft spins fast and turns a larger gearwheel attached to the wheel more slowly. This reduced speed gives more turning power or spinning force, called torque. So the robot can travel up hills or carry heavier loads.

DO YOU KNOW?

(ROBOTS DO)

Talking torque

A mobile robot relies on its electric motor. This makes its strongest turning force or torque when it is spinning fast. The problem is that the robot needs the most turning force to start it moving when it is still. Really clever robots feed more electricity into their motor when they start up, then reduce the amount as the robot speeds up. This gives a smoother ride and saves lots of battery power.

▶▶ *The engines of big trucks and railway trains have massive gears to adjust the spinning speed and turning power (torque). Robots have smaller versions for the same purpose.*

ROBO-FUTURE

Step into the future

Scientists and engineers are always developing motors that last longer and use less energy. Small motors that turn around slowly and precisely, called stepper motors, are used for computer disc drives. Bigger, stronger versions would be a good choice for the newest robot designs.

Robo-batteries

Small robots have rechargeable battery packs, similar to the ones in mobile phones and mp3 players. Bigger robots need larger batteries, like those designed for cars or trucks. At the end of every session these robots need to be plugged into the electricity supply for a few hours. Solar-bots have solar panels that turn light into electricity. They can go on for longer, charging their own batteries – provided it is daytime.

▶▶ *The tortoise lawnmower runs on solar power and charges its batteries by sunlight. It detects objects in its way and the lawn edge, to stay on the grass and out of trouble.*

Toy robots need a regular recharge or they run down and 'die'.

11

Finding the way

As we walk about, we automatically see objects in our way and avoid them. For a mobile robot, this is a great challenge. It needs to know where it is, where it's going, and find the way – this is known as **navigation**. It has to steer carefully and safely, and avoid danger, bashes and crashes.

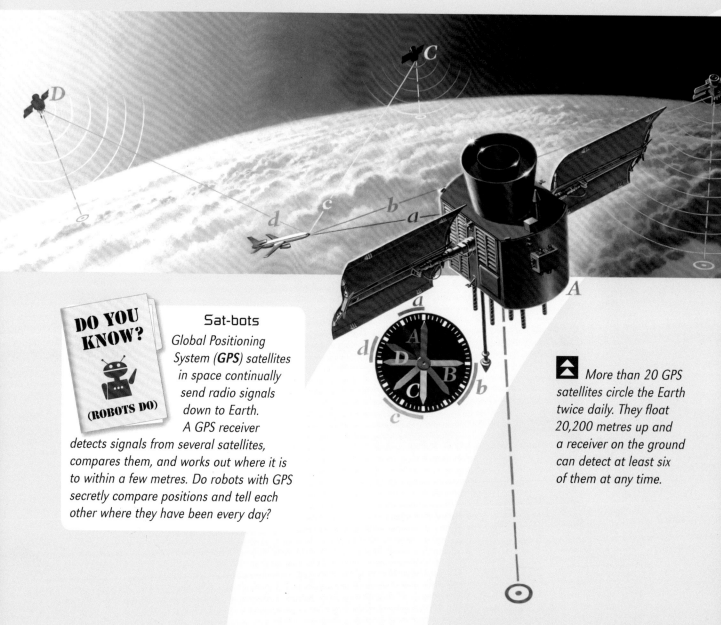

DO YOU KNOW?

(ROBOTS DO)

Sat-bots
*Global Positioning System (**GPS**) satellites in space continually send radio signals down to Earth. A GPS receiver detects signals from several satellites, compares them, and works out where it is to within a few metres. Do robots with GPS secretly compare positions and tell each other where they have been every day?*

▲ *More than 20 GPS satellites circle the Earth twice daily. They float 20,200 metres up and a receiver on the ground can detect at least six of them at any time.*

What's around?
Robots have many **sensors**. Humans have sensors too – our eyes and ears. Some robots have camera eyes which detect light around them and send the information to an onboard computer. This works out which objects it needs to avoid from their shapes and colours. If an object gradually grows larger in the camera's view, the robot works out that it is moving towards it.

Invisible beams

Some robots have simpler ways of detecting nearby objects. They send out short bursts or **pulses** of beams, especially **laser beams** or invisible **infrared light** (the same as the beams used in TV remote controls). Laser or infrared sensors pick up any beams that bounce back, or reflect, from objects nearby. The direction and timing of the reflections shows the size, shape and distance of the object.

Where am I going?

Robots that move around the same area all the time usually have a map in their computer memory. Once they detect three or four familiar objects nearby, such as walls, machines, desks or trees, they can work out where they are. Their computer program can then instruct them on how to steer to the destination. Bigger outdoor mobile robots usually have satellite navigation.

Outdoor robots such as Navigator rely on satellite navigation. If the GPS receiver fails, the robot stops.

Robo-blog ■

OOPS!

'This morning I got into trouble. I was taking some supplies along the corridor as usual, and I almost bumped into a new cupboard. My human programmer hadn't put the cupboard into my computer memory map. So I didn't know it was there. Luckily my front pressure bar touched it and I stopped in time.'■

Many modern cars have a GPS or satnav (satellite navigation) receiver.

Robots on the road

Imagine it's the rush-hour in a big city. Traffic jams build up, drivers get annoyed, cyclists weave in and out, and people run between vehicles. Travelling by robo-car sounds like a good idea to take the strain out of driving. But could a robot cope with so much going on?

▲ *Busy roads mean human drivers must be alert to all kinds of sights and sounds. Robot drivers are not yet clever or safe enough for these conditions.*

▶▶ *The Pivo 2 car of the future has a camera eye and microphone ear to check its human driver's face and voice. When the driver shows signs of stress, such as frowning or shouting, the little robot head suggests a break to calm down.*

Smart cars

Although fully robotic cars are a long way off, cars grow smarter every year. Sensors warn the driver when other vehicles come too close. Smart nav systems can learn a driver's regular routes and habits, and look out for mistakes. They can also listen for traffic warnings on local radio, TV and emergency channels, and help the driver choose another route.

Way to go

A completely robotic car that drives itself on public roads, obeys traffic signs and signals, and avoids other vehicles and hazards, is probably many years away. There are simply too many actions to carry out and problems that might happen, such as a child running into the road. On public roads, safety is the biggest concern, and today's robots are not quick thinking or reliable enough to travel on these roads. However robot style gadgets can help drivers in many ways. Some modern cars have breakdown warning systems, obstacle sensor beepers and automatic parking controls. Intelligent satellite navigation can be programmed into the steering wheel so the driver feels which way to go while staying in control.

Auto-trucks

Away from public roads, in places with less traffic such as quarries, mines and industrial sites, robo-vehicles are becoming more common. Some of the biggest are huge mining trucks that weigh more than 500 tonnes – 12 times heavier than the biggest trucks on ordinary roads. They find their way by **satnav** and come to a quick stop if anything goes wrong.

An assisted parking device uses ultrasound sensors to detect the road edge and other vehicles, then shows the driver the best parking method.

DO YOU KNOW?

(ROBOTS DO)

Robot road cones

Lines of road cones, barriers and bollards mean roadworks or an accident ahead. Engineers are testing mobile versions with batteries and wheels, which can detect their position using radio signals. They are programmed to move about and take up an exact pattern, for example, to close off a lane for safety as soon as a car breaks down. But could they communicate with each other by radio and move about by themselves?

Ultimate challenge

One of the world's toughest robot contests is called the Grand Challenge, held every few years in America. The contest is for robot cars without drivers and the prizes are worth millions of dollars.

Ghost town

The US Defense Advanced Research Projects Agency (DARPA), tests all kinds of weird and wacky ideas that might come in useful one day. Its Grand Challenge is held in a remote part of the Mojave Desert in California.

In 2007 DARPA held an urban challenge which had a route through a 'city' – an air force base which had been closed down. The driverless robots faced challenges such as travelling over rough ground, steering between buildings, parking, avoiding other cars and people (in the form of cardboard cut-outs) and moving through traffic.

In the 2007 Challenge Lone Wolf (above) reverses to turn around while Talos (right) drives carefully along a pretend city street. Lone Wolf is a modified Lotus Elise with eight laser sensors. Talos is a Landrover LR3 with 13 laser sensors, 15 radar sensors and five video cameras.

Failed challenger

The DARPA Challenge car Alice became a star because it failed in a big way. The car was a modified Ford E350 van built by CalTech (California Institute of Technology). The car's satnav went wrong and Alice roared over a concrete barrier towards nearby spectators. But the human safety back-up crew flicked the 'kill' switch before Alice did any real damage.

Challenge entrants

The robot that wins the Grand Challenge scores highest on speed, carrying out all the tasks and staying out of trouble. The vehicles control themselves for up to ten hours with no human help. They have all kinds of sensors, including laser and infrared beams, cameras, the radio signals of radar, and satnav. Powerful electric motors work the steering wheel, throttle (accelerator) and brakes. The 'brain' of the vehicle is a powerful computer that works out where to go and how fast, and which part of the challenge to try next. There are many built-in safety features to make sure the vehicles don't race off on their own across the desert.

Serious business

Robot designers and engineers spend years and lots of money developing and building their robot cars, because the challenge has a serious side. It helps to develop robot military vehicles which could carry supplies in war zones, or even fight an enemy through city streets. This might save the lives of many soldiers.

▼ *The robot Chevrolet Tahoe named Boss won the 2007 Challenge, completing the course in four hours and ten minutes. Its human team from Carnegie Mellon University and General Motors won the first prize of $2 million.*

Robots on rails

Robot trains and other vehicles that run on railway lines can only go where the rails take them. Even so, they must start and stop properly, control their speed, obey signals and make sure they take the correct track where sets of rails meet at points.

Robot trains carry passengers to and fro at many main airports, seaports, theme parks and other large sites. These trains are at Beijing Airport, China. Passengers can press an emergency button if there's a problem.

No drivers
Several cities around the world have driverless railway train systems, including Beijing in China, Yongin in South Korea, Kuala Lumpur in Malaysia, Vancouver and Toronto in Canada, and Las Vegas, Detroit and New York in the USA. They are called rapid mass transit, which means that the robot trains carry lots of people quickly around the city and nearby, often on lines raised above the streets. Driverless trains also haul wagons in quarries, mines and factories.

Signs of trouble
Driverless trains have onboard computers programmed with their routes and station stops. They also have satnav and similar gadgets, and radio links to a central control room. On-train sensors record speed and direction, whether there are problems with the motors, wheels or other parts, and even how much shaking or vibration there is, which could reveal a cracked rail or chipped wheel.

Central control

All the information from the train sensors is updated and sent to central control. Here people keep an eye on the whole train network. Each time a train stops at a station, its equipment is checked automatically. In addition, sensors along the tracks detect each train's passing, the time and how fast it is going.

Safe systems

Wherever people and robots get together, safety is vital. On a robot railway, if one part breaks down or fails, there are at least two back-ups ready to take over. If a train runs over an accidentally broken rail, the track signals automatically stop other trains coming near. The system is designed to be failsafe. Even if the electricity supply fails, the people and trains stay safe.

 In a robot railway control room, people keep a constant check on the trains, signals, points and video cameras, to make sure everything is working properly.

Robot trains often travel above city streets, away from cars and people. The Las Vegas Monorail in Nevada, USA, has a track more than six kilometres long.

ROBOT SUPERSTAR

Train pusher

Few robots match Elbrams for size and power. Each Elbram is an automatic train pusher that weighs more than 50 tonnes. It runs on rails and has diesel engines and two arms worked by **hydraulics**. One arm grabs the rail and pushes along, then lets go as the other one takes over, and so on. It's like pulling hand over hand on a rope. Slowly Elbram can roll along a whole train weighing 10,000 tonnes.

The sky's the limit

'Hello, this is your **autopilot** George speaking. Today I will be flying you across the ocean while the human pilots have a snack and a nap. Don't worry, we work as a team and do it every day.'

Help in the cockpit

Robot autopilots do not have total control in planes that carry people. They help the human pilots. Big passenger planes have an autopilot which is part of the computer-based flight management system (FMS). This works out where the plane is, where it is going, and the best route to avoid storms and other dangers. Once the human pilots have set the autopilot they can relax. But they still keep an eye on the controls and displays, just in case anything goes wrong. Lights flash and beepers sound if there is a problem.

Knowing the way

An autopilot uses a satnav system as one source of information. Radio beacons on the ground that send out coded radio signals about their location are another source. Most planes also have an inertial navigation system (INS) which contains machines that measure the plane's speed and direction very accurately (see page 21).

▼ Once the autopilot is set on a modern passenger plane, the flight crew can spend time planning ahead or double-checking that all is well.

The Heron robot spy plane carries several kinds of cameras and other sensors. It is about the size of a two-seater aircraft and can stay in the sky for more than two days.

Taking measurements

How does INS work? If you are in a car that suddenly goes faster, or accelerates, you are pressed back in your seat. As you turn a corner, you tend to lean sideways. INS **accelerometers** measure a plane's speed and changes of direction very accurately, second by second. There is also usually a **gyroscope** – a fast-spinning wheel or ball that stays in a steady position, always pointing the same way as the aircraft turns, rises or goes down. The computer combines information from these INS devices to work out how far the plane has travelled and in which direction.

Planes without pilots

Some aircraft have no pilots at all. They are fully robotic or **autonomous**, guided by an onboard computer using satnav information. These types of robo-planes include military spy **drones** that take photographs of army headquarters, air bases and naval ports.

In the comedy film Airplane (1980) the autopilot is called Otto rather than George – and he's an inflatable dummy rather than a real pilot.

ROBOT SUPERSTAR

George

The autopilot of an airplane is traditionally known as George. This might be after George DeBeeson who improved autopilot design in the 1920s. Or it could refer to the gyroscope part of the autopilot. In the alphabet pilots use, the word Golf stands for the letter G, but the word for G used to be George. The pilot said, 'Let George do it', meaning that the gyroscope autopilot was taking over.

Robo-boats

Robot watercraft on rivers, lakes and seas face many dangers. They could hit rocks, get stuck in the shallows, bump into another boat, capsize or even sink beneath the waves...

ROBOT OR NOT?

Self-steering

Some boats have self-steering or autohelm, like a simple autopilot. The crew set the angle between a flag-like wind vane and the steering rudder. If the boat changes course, a lever system moves the rudder so the boat turns back to the correct angle. There are also versions with a magnetic compass and GPS. But these are not real robots. They cannot decide to change course, start or stop, detect when the wind direction alters, or avoid obstacles. However, they do give the boat crew a rest.

Cruising the ocean

Beagle B is three and a half metres long and can travel for weeks on a course programmed into its computer. This robot sailing dinghy detects the strength and direction of the wind and the depth of the water it is floating in using echo-sounding or sonar. It can also work out whether it is upright or leaning. *Beagle B* has a magnetic compass and a GPS satnav receiver, as well as solar panels which charge its batteries. These power the computer and the electric motors that move the rudder and sail.

The robot sailing dinghy Beagle B *cruises around taking water samples to test in its onboard mini-laboratory.*

Across the Atlantic?

Pinta, Roboboat Mark III and other small robotic boats are designed to sail all the way across the Atlantic Ocean in about three months. Most of them have sails, an onboard computer and solar panels for electricity. They are testing the idea that one day large sailing ships could carry cargoes across the ocean without a crew or fuel.

Cleaner means faster

Seaweed and small sea creatures such as limpets and barnacles grow on the hulls of ships and boats. Cleaning them off allows boats to go faster and use less fuel. The small robot cleaner HISMAR (hull identification system for marine autonomous robotics) crawls over the hull of boats, blasting off growths with powerful water jets. The cleaner works out the quickest route to clean the hull while avoiding parts such as the propeller or water intakes.

▼ *Cleaning ship and boat hulls usually means they must come out of the water in a dry dock. Robot hull cleaners work while the boat is still in the water.*

Move like an animal

The most successful movers in the animal world are insects. There are millions of different kinds, all with six legs. Spiders, with eight legs, also go almost everywhere. Snakes and worms may be legless, but they are great movers too. Robots can copy all these creatures.

Stand up, fall over

Six legs or more on a robot are useful because even if three lift off the ground, the others keep the robot well balanced and stable. The robot moves a few legs at a time and steps along without falling over. If a robot had four legs – one at each corner – it would topple if it lifted even one of the legs. Successful four-legged (or quadruped) robots can bend their other three legs to tilt the body over them and stay standing. This type of robot needs delicate balance sensors which can detect the downward pull of **gravity** and how much the robot tilts or leans. The sensors are connected to fast-acting electric motors that work the legs.

▶▶ *The Genghis series of mini-robots is designed to test different ways of walking. One of the most successful designs has six legs, like the real insect shown here, which is a cricket.*

Ninja is a four-legged robot with 20 suckers on each foot. These allow it to climb smooth surfaces and even crawl up windows, to check the glass and other items such as wires and pipes.

Robo-blog■

METAL MUSCLES

'Hi, Robo-lobster calling. I'm as big as a
big real-life lobster and I crawl along the
seabed on my eight legs to detect explosive
mines. But I don't have electric motors
like ordinary robots. I have metal muscles!
They are shape-shifting wires that get
shorter when electricity passes through
them. When the electricity stops, the wires
lengthen again. This moves my legs in the
same pattern of movement as a real lobster.
I must crawl off to work now, so I'll finish
my Robo-lob-blog.'■

Running robots

Walk over there, run back here, jog for a while, hop and skip, leap and jump. We humans can move in many ways on two legs or even one – it's so natural and easy. But for robots, bipedal or two-legged travel is an enormous problem.

In the balance

We humans have a very good sense of balance and our muscles react quickly, so we don't fall over even when we stand on one leg. We are, in effect, one-legged for about two-thirds of the time when walking, because we lift up each foot in turn and move it forwards. It's tricky to build a robot with gravity detectors, accelerators and other sensors that are delicate enough, and work fast enough, to power electric motors and move mechanical legs as quickly as human ones.

Small and simple

Runbot is a small robot less than 30 centimetres tall. It is two legs and not much else. Each hip has a small electric motor, and so does each knee. There are sensors to measure the angles of these joints, how upright Runbot is, and how hard each foot presses down. The angle or slope of the ground is measured by an infrared beam.

Leaning to walk

A clever feature of Runbot is its 'brain'. This is not one single computer but several sets of electronic **circuits** and **microchips**. If Runbot takes small steps and starts to lean forward too far, the circuits work together to detect this and lengthen its stride. In this way Runbot can learn to walk and run, go uphill and down, and cope with uneven ground.

◀◀ *A toddler shows that humans find learning to walk quite difficult and have plenty of trips and falls. Bipedal robots have similar problems.*

The two-legged robot Denise (the knees) tests out new kinds of leg joints and balance sensors. Walking robots have improved hugely in the past ten years.

ROBOT OR NOT?

Extra power

The human body has a framework of bones inside called an **endoskeleton** (meaning skeleton inside). Robot engineers make bigger frameworks of metal and plastic called **exoskeletons** (meaning skeleton outside), like a mechanical suit to fit around the person's head, body, arms and legs. As the human inside moves, the exoskeleton copies the actions but with much greater strength, using powerful electric motors or even a car engine! Are these powered exoskeletons true robots? Not really – they are under human control and don't work by themselves or make decisions.

This exoskeleton is worn by divers underwater. It gives them extra strength to help them move heavy objects.

Going places

Mobile robots move in very strange ways even when they fall over! Tetwalkers look like pyramids made of tubes with three sides and a base. They change shape by making their tubes shorter or longer which lets them move by toppling or somersaulting along.

Four-sided robot

A single tetwalker has four sides, each one a triangle. This shape is called a **tetrahedron**, hence the name tetwalker. The sides are made of hollow tubes that slide into each other so they can shorten or lengthen, like telescopes. Electric motors at the corners where the sides join, or in the middle of each side, make this happen.

Robo-blog■

TUMBLE-TETS

'Here we go, tumbling along. Nanotets on the move, singing our song. We do lots of jobs, we carry and measure. We test and experiment, we even find treasure. If one of us breaks, the others work harder. Forget stupid humans — nanotets forever!'■

▶▶ Somersaulting robots have strong, soft rubber cushions on each corner, to soften their tumbles. This cubewalker has eight sides, each one a square.

Shape-shifter

When a tetwalker moves, three sides become longer while the other shortens. The tetwalker grows taller, leans to one side and flops over. The sides change their lengths again, and the same thing happens. It's not so much tetwalking as tet-tumbling. A computer controls the electric motors. By changing which sides grow longer or shorter, the tetwalker can alter direction, zigzag or go into reverse. And it can cope with lumps and bumps, soft ground such as sand or loose pebbles, as well as slopes.

Tiny tets

In the future lots of very tiny tetwalkers called **nanotets** could be linked into groups or swarms, all tumbling along together. Their small onboard computers could also be linked. If the leading members of the group came upon a blockage or obstacle, the computers would decide between them which way they should all steer to go round it. These huge groups could become self-controlling or autonomous, known as ANTS – autonomous nanotechnology swarms.

 Tetwalkers are being tested as robots to send into space. They could move across rough ground on other planets, unlike the usual wheeled rovers.

ROBO-FUTURE

Better GPS

European space scientists are building a new satnav system called Galileo. This should allow ships, boats, planes, cars and trains find their position to the nearest metre, rather than several metres as with GPS. In a few years robots could use both GPS and Galileo to know where they are and navigate much more precisely.

Glossary of robo-terms

accelerometer
A device or gadget that measures movement, especially how quickly something speeds up (accelerates) or slows down (decelerates).

autonomous
A machine or device that mainly controls itself and works on its own, without human control, as most robots do.

autopilot
Automatic pilot – a machine that steers and controls an aircraft for a set amount of time, but which can be switched off if there is a problem, so human pilots can take over.

circuit
In electrical equipment, a circuit is the path or route of electricity through various wires, switches, microchips and other parts.

cog
A wheel with pointed teeth around the edge, sometimes called a gearwheel or cogwheel, found on bicycles and in many robots (see gears).

drones
Robot planes with no human crew which people program or instruct to fly to a specific place, perhaps to take photographs or to spy on others.

endoskeleton
A strong supporting framework on the inside of an animal or machine, such as the skeleton of bones inside the human body.

exoskeleton
A strong supporting framework on the outside of an animal or machine, such as the hard outer body casing of a beetle.

gears
Two or more wheels with pointed teeth around the edges, called cogs, cogwheels or gearwheels. They have teeth that interlock or mesh together so that one wheel turns the next (see cog).

GPS
Stands for Global Positioning System: this is made up of more than 20 satellites which travel round the Earth and send out radio signals detected by a GPS receiver. They show the position, or location, of the receiver and help to find the way or navigate. GPS is often called satnav (see navigation).

gravity
The natural pulling force that affects all objects, from pieces of dust to stars, and attracts other objects. The bigger or more massive an object, the stronger its gravity.

gyroscope
A very fast-spinning wheel or ball that resists being moved or tilted and tries to stay in the same position.

hydraulics
A system worked by a liquid under pressure, such as oil or water pumped into a pipe that creates a pushing force at the other end.

infrared light
Light with waves slightly longer than red light waves, which our eyes cannot see, but which some animals' eyes can. Used in gadgets such as remote-control switches for TVs and robots.

laser beams
Beams of very powerful light that do not spread out or widen, unlike ordinary light beams.

locomotory robots
Robots that locomote or move about, travelling from one place to another rather than staying in the same place.

microchip
A small wafer or flat piece of a substance such as silicon, with thousands of microscopic electronic parts on its surface.

nanotets
Very tiny tetrahedrons (see tetrahedron), even smaller than the dot on this 'i'.

navigation
Finding the way or route while travelling on a journey from one place to another.

pneumatic tyres
Hollow tyres filled with air under high pressure, like those on bicycles and cars.

pivot
Swing around or tilt or spin.

pulses
Short bursts or amounts with gaps between, like a light that flashes on and off many times.

reduction gears
Gearwheels that reduce spinning or turning speed, when a small gearwheel with few teeth links or meshes with a large gearwheel with many teeth. This makes the large wheel turn more slowly than the small one (see gears).

satnav
A short form of satellite navigation, meaning finding the way using a GPS receiver that detects radio signals from satellites going around the Earth (see GPS and navigation).

sensors
Devices that detect something, such as light, sound, touch, heat or certain chemicals.

tetrahedron
A shape with four flat sides, each of which is a triangle.

torque
Turning or twisting power or strength.

ultrasound
Sounds that are too high-pitched and shrill for human ears, so we cannot hear them, but which some animals and gadgets can detect.

Further reading

Robots by Clive Gifford (Carlton Books 2008)

Building Robots with LEGO Mindstorms NXT by Mario Ferrari (Syngress 2007)

Robot by Roger Bridgman (DK Eyewitness Books 2004)

Learn About Robotics (Sci Faxes) by De-Ann Black (Top That! 2005)

Robots and Robotics series: How Robots Work and other titles by Tony Hyland (Macmillan Library, Nelson Thornes 2008)

Ultimate Robot by Robert Malone (Dorling Kindersley 2004)

Websites

Robot World News
This site covers the top news stories on robotics, artificial intelligence and related areas, but it also has more fun information on robots such as toys.
http://www.robotworldnews.com/robots4u.html

Robot video clips
Video clips of all kinds of robots in action.
http://www.robotclips.com/

Robot Wars
In the popular Robot Wars competitions, teams strive to improve robots of all kinds, not just for battle – see especially the SAFETY page.
http://www.ukrobotwars.com/mains.htm

Index